The Roman Empire

Written by Robin Twiddy
Designed by Jasmine Pointer

BookLife PUBLISHING

©This edition published 2023. First published in 2022.
BookLife Publishing Ltd.
King's Lynn, Norfolk, PE30 4LS, UK

ISBN 978-1-80155-159-5

All rights reserved. Printed in Poland.
A catalogue record for this book is available from the British Library.

The Roman Empire
Written by Robin Twiddy
Designed by Jasmine Pointer

An Introduction to Accessible Readers...

Our 'really readable' Accessible Readers have been specifically created to support the reading development of young readers with learning differences, such as dyslexia.

Our aim is to share our love of books with children, providing the same learning and developmental opportunities to every child.

INCREASED FONT SIZE AND SPACING improves readability and ensures text feels much less crowded.

OFF-WHITE BACKGROUNDS ON MATTE PAPER improves text contrast and avoids dazzling readers.

SIMPLIFIED PAGE LAYOUT reduces distractions and aids concentration.

CAREFULLY CRAFTED along guidelines set out in the British Dyslexia Association's Dyslexia-Friendly Style Guide.

Images courtesy of Shutterstock.com. Cover – joserpizzaro, WindVector, Vladimir Sazonov, Yaroslaff, zarenata. 4–5 – leoks, AlexZaitsev. 6–7 – Anna Jurkovska, meunierd. 8–9 – Deatonphotos, Florin Cnejevici. 10–11 – meunierd. 12–13 – Sergej Razvodovskij, cosma. 14–15 – Xseon, pcruciatti. 16–17 – Luis Pizarro Ruiz, KinoAlyse. 18–19 – mojahata, Thanantorn Kainet. 20–21 – Maljalen, Massimo Todaro. 22–23 – WindVector, Charly Morlock. 24–25 – Fernando Cortes, Antonio Ciero Reina. 26–27 – Artem Mishukov, lucianop. 28–29 – Spartacusrsl, Paolo Gallo.

Contents

Page 4   The Romans

Page 8   The Roman Army

Page 12   Weapons

Page 16   Roman Gods and Goddesses

Page 22   The Circus

Page 26   Emperors

Page 30   Index

Page 31   The Roman Empire: Quiz

The Romans

The Romans lived over 2,000 years ago and could be found in many countries around the world. We can still see evidence of this now, such as the aqueducts.

The Romans were good at making lots of things, such as roads. Lots of the things that they made are still around now.

Roman roads are known for being very straight. The roads were very important for the Romans. The roads helped the Romans move their armies around.

The Romans built straight roads because they knew that it was quicker to travel in a straight line. It was also safer. Enemies could be hiding around corners.

The Roman Army

The Roman Empire was big thanks to its strong armies. They trained hard to become good at fighting. When they defeated other armies, those armies joined the Roman Empire.

Roman armies spread from Rome in modern-day Italy to many countries. They conquered the rest of Italy, Greece, Spain, France, the North African coast, much of the Middle East, Britain and more.

The Roman armies had better equipment than other armies at the time. Their equipment and their training gave them the upper hand in fights.

The Romans had better shields than most other armies that they met. They used them along with other shields in a big group to defend themselves from arrows.

Weapons

The shields were made to fit with other shields without any gaps. By using their shields like this, the Romans could move across a field raining with arrows without getting hit.

One of the main weapons used by the Roman army was the gladius. The gladius was a short sword with a double-sided blade.

The pulim is the name for the long spears that Roman soldiers carried. When they were thrown at the enemy, they would stick into their shields and bend.

The bent spears were hard to pull out, making the enemy shields useless. Roman Soldiers would carry two of these spears into battle.

Roman Gods and Goddesses

The Romans had lots of gods and goddesses, and they all did different things. There was a goddess of harvest. Romans prayed to her asking for good food to grow in the fields.

The Romans gave offerings. They believed that if they did this, the god or goddess might help them in their lives. Some offerings were grapes or grain.

Jupiter was the king of the gods and the god of the sky, lightning and thunder. The Romans believed that Jupiter watched over them and would be angered if a vow or promise was broken.

The Romans had gods and goddesses for nearly everything. Cardea was the Roman goddess of door handles and hinges. The Romans believed she stopped evil spirits from entering their homes.

Laverna was the Roman goddess of thieves and mischief. The Romans used to believe that she spent all her time tricking the people in the Roman Empire.

Thieves were often punished in Rome. They might have had to pay back more money than what they had stolen. Some thieves were killed as a warning to other thieves.

The Circus

The Romans liked to go to the circus. The circus was an open-air place that lots of events were held at. Crowds watched races and fights at the circus.

The circus was where gladiators would fight to entertain the people of Rome. Gladiators were slaves, servants or criminals trained to fight to the death.

Gladiators would sometimes race chariots or even fight animals. Some of the animals that gladiators were known to fight are panthers, lions, giraffes and tigers.

It was free to go to the circus. For many Romans it was the only chance they had to see the emperor. The rich would sit up high in the arena.

Emperors

The Roman Empire was ruled by an emperor. The emperor was the highest power in the land. He could make rules and told the armies what to do and where to go.

The first emperor of Rome was called Caesar Augustus. But there were many more emperors after him. Some were very good rulers and ruled Rome in times of peace.

Augustus, Claudius and Trajan were all emperors that made the Roman empire bigger by leading armies into other countries. They made these countries part of the empire.

The most famous ruler of Rome was Julius Caesar. Julius Caesar was never an emperor; he was a general who took control of Rome with his army. His nephew was Caesar Augustus, the first emperor of Rome.

Index:

animals 24

Caesar, Julius 24

Jupiter 18

shields 11–12

swords 13

The Roman Empire: Quiz

1. Who was the first emperor of Rome?

2. Why did the Romans build such straight roads?

3. Who would sit up high at the circus?

4. Can you use the Index page to find out how Romans used their shields?

5. What do you think it would be like to visit a Roman circus?

Helpful Hints for Reading at Home

This 'really readable' Accessible Reader has been carefully written and designed to help children with learning differences whether they are reading in the classroom or at home. However, there are some extra ways in which you can help your child at home.

- Try to provide a quiet space for your child to read, with as few distractions as possible.

- Try to allow your child as much time as they need to decode the letters and words on the page.

- Reading with a learning difference can be frustrating and difficult. Try to let your child take short, managed breaks between reading sessions if they begin to feel frustrated.

- Build your child's confidence with positive praise and encouragement throughout.

- Your child's teacher, as well as many charities, can provide you with lots of tips and techniques to help your child read at home.